Tractor-Trailer
Trucker

A Powerful Truck Book

Tractor-Trailer
Trucker

A Powerful Truck Book

Joyce Slayton Mitchell

Photographs by Steven Borns

Tricycle Press
Berkeley, California

Sources and Acknowledgements

For teaching us everything we know about trucking, we would like to thank the following people: Joe Bellavance, president of A. Bellavance Trucking, Inc.; his son, operations manager Roland Bellavance, who so generously gave his time and expertise, and allowed us access to others in his company; dispatchers David Bellavance and Richard Dufresne; Ann M. Wakefield, resource librarian of the American Trucking Association; Mary Venditta, of Corporate Affairs of Mack Trucks; and Nick Robinson, driver for Yellow Freight System, Inc. We are especially grateful to tractor-trailer trucker Ken Blair of Hardwick, Vermont, and want to acknowledge his professionalism and dedication to a 3-million-mile, 30-year career of life on the road. We thank him for generously sharing 6,703 miles of it with photographer Steven Borns.

Finally, we want to enthusiastically express our appreciation to Tricycle Press publisher Nicole Geiger and editor Cybele Knowles for providing their editorial guidance and a teamwork environment for this exciting project: *Tractor-Trailer Trucker.*

UNDER THE HOOD

Before starting out, check oil, water, and coolant levels. Check hoses and fan belts. When the belts are new, check for tightness. As belts get older, check for cracks, fraying, and slackness.

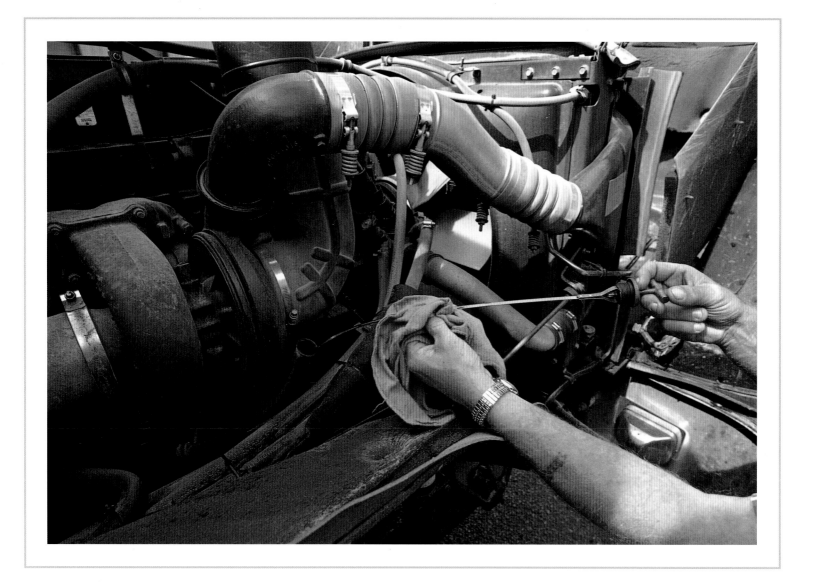

OIL AND WATER

Check oil level with the dipstick. The oil must be changed every 20,000 miles. If the engine starts to overheat due to oil or water leaks while you are driving, a warning light on your control panel will come on. You then have 30 to 40 seconds to find a safe parking spot before the engine automatically shuts down as a safety measure.

CHECK THE SHOCKS

The shock absorber is under the fifth wheel of the tractor. Check shock absorber mounts and the mounting eyes at each end of the shock. Look for fluid leakage: check for oil stains on the sides of the shock absorber tubes.

HOOK UP TRACTOR AND TRAILER

Make sure fifth-wheel jaws are open. Back tractor as squarely as possible at the center of the trailer until fifth-wheel jaws engage the kingpin on the trailer. Check that fifth-wheel jaws have closed completely around trailer kingpin. Make sure that no daylight shows between the fifth wheel and the trailer's deck plate. Perform a pull test—pulling forward with the trailer brakes set—to check the coupling.

HOOK UP LIGHT LINE AND BRAKE LINES

Hook up trailer light line and brake lines, and check connections for air leaks on the brake lines. Secure lines properly to prevent tangling or chafing.

LOAD

Load cargo at the warehouse, and then check in with the dispatcher for trucking orders.

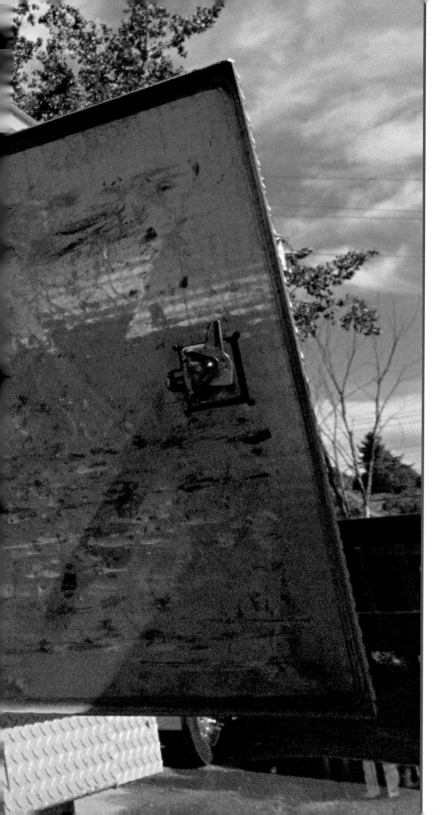

CHAINS AND STRAPS

Carry extra chains and straps, since cargo can shift during the long drive. The storage rack holds 2-inch straps, 4-inch straps, chains, ratchet binders, winch binders, bungees, and felt and plastic corner protectors.

TRACTOR-TRAILER TIRES

Good tires help you steer well and support the heavy weight of the load. Measure the depth of the tire tread with a tire-depth gauge, or for a quick check, use a dime. New tires have a tread of $18/32$ of an inch. When the front tire treads get worn down to $4/32$ of an inch, tires must be changed. Change tires after 100,000 to 120,000 miles.

AIRBAGS

Check airbags under trailer for visual signs of damage. Airbags balance the cargo load and make the trailer weight even for a smooth and safe ride.

THREE-POINT STANCE

Be sure of foothold and handhold when entering and exiting the cab. Use a three-point stance: two feet on the steps and one hand on the handhold. Remember that steps, handhold, gratings, and fuel tank tops can be extra slippery when oily.

GEARS

There are 8 to 18 gears in an 18-wheeler. This tractor has 13 gears. Gears 1 to 5 are the low gears, and 6 to 13 are the high gears.

Move the stick shift to change from gear to gear. Press the black button on the stick shift to change from the low gears to the high gears. Within the high gears, press the red button (the split-switcher) to shift half a gear. Select gear 13 to cruise at the speed limit on interstate highways.

START ENGINE AND CHECK EMERGENCY EQUIPMENT

Start engine and set at low idle for warm-up. Check for abnormal engine noise. Check gauges for normal readings. Check horns and windshield wipers pre-trip and post-trip. Check steering-wheel action. Test all lights, including four-way flasher switch for turn signals.

CHECK AIR BRAKES

Put trailer air supply valve in "normal." Step on brake pedal to apply and release brakes. Pump brakes and check readings. A normal reading is 90 to 120 pounds per square inch (psi). When the air pressure falls below 60 psi, "low air" warnings will activate and all brakes will automatically lock as a safety measure.

Drive.

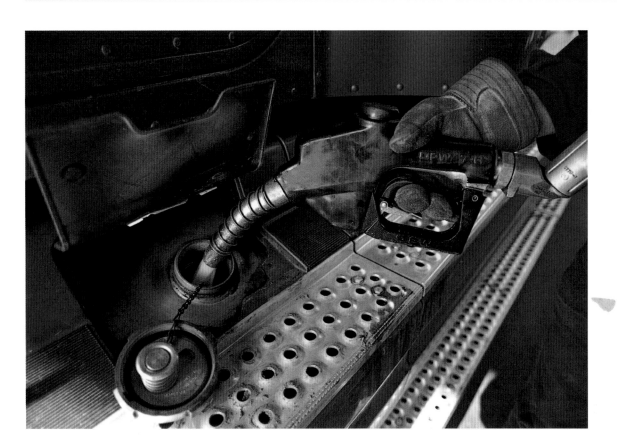

FILL UP

Each fuel tank holds 100 to 150 gallons. There are two tanks on an 18-wheeler. Check both tanks every day. Big tractor-trailers get 5.5 miles per gallon.

SATELLITE PAGING

Use satellite paging system to check schedule and destination goals.

CIRCLE CHECK

Do a circle check before climbing back into the tractor. Walk around your rig checking for damage and loose connections. Kick tires to check air pressure. Complete the vehicle inspection report in your daily log.

The Official Trucker's Daily Log

				/		/		

DATE (MONTH / DAY / YEAR)

DRIVER MILES

VEHICLE NUMBERS

DRIVER ID(S)

COMPANY

CO-DRIVER NAME

MAIN ADDRESS

	Mid-night	1	2	3	4	5	6	7	8	9	10	11	Noon	1	2	3	4	5	6	7	8	9	10	11	TOTALS
1. OFF DUTY																										
2. SLEEPING																										
3. DRIVING																										
4. ON DUTY (not driving)																										

SIGNATURE / CERTIFICATION

Number of off-duty hours INCLUDING today: ____

Totals MUST add up to 24 hours.

SHIPMENTS ON BOARD

ORDER NO.	WEIGHT	FROM	TO

MILES DRIVEN TODAY BY STATES

STATE	LOADED	EMPTY	FUEL PURCHASED TICKETS ATTACHED
			GALS.
			GALS.
			GALS.
			GALS.
			GALS.
			GALS.
TOTAL			

DRIVER'S VEHICLE INSPECTION REPORT

DRIVER USE ✓ IF SATISFACTORY
USE ✗ IF UNSATISFACTORY

MECHANIC USE ✓ WHEN CORRECTED AND YOUR INITIALS

TRACTOR/TRUCK NO. _____

TRAILOR(S) NO.(S) _____

D – DRIVER'S REPORT / M – MECHANIC'S REPORT	D	M
Brake Lines _____		
Electric Lines _____		
Drive Line _____		
Coupling Devices_____		
Tires, Wheels, Rims _____		
Suspension System_____		
Body _____		
Glass _____		
Exhaust _____		
Frame and Assembly _____		
Fuel System _____		
Cooling System _____		
Engine _____		
Leaks _____		
Head Lights _____		
Tail Lights _____		
Stop and Turn Lights _____		
Clearance and Marker Lights _____		
Reflectors _____		
Air Pressure Warning Device _____		
Oil Pressure _____		
Ammeter _____		
Horn _____		
Windshield Wipers _____		
Parking Brakes _____		
Clutch _____		
Transmission _____		
Rear Vision Mirror _____		
Steering _____		
Service Brakes _____		
Speedometer _____		
Other Items _____		

D – DRIVER'S REPORT / M – MECHANIC'S REPORT	D	M
EMERGENCY EQUIPMENT		
Reflective Triangles _____		
Fire Extinguisher_____		
Flags, Fumes, Fuses, Spare Bulbs _____		
Tire Chains _____		
Brakes _____		
Brake Connections _____		
Coupling Devices_____		
Kingpin _____		
Doors _____		
Hitch _____		
Landing Gear _____		
Roof _____		
Suspension System_____		
Tarpaulin _____		
Other _____		

I MADE INSPECTION AS REQUIRED ON LISTED ITEMS

DRIVER: _____
DATE

ODOMETER END OF DAY: _____
ODOMETER START OF DAY: _____
TOTAL MILES DRIVEN TODAY: _____
NEXT LUBRICATION DUE AT: _____
MILEAGE

☐ ABOVE DEFECTS CORRECTED
☐ ABOVE DEFECTS NEED NOT BE CORRECTED FOR SAFE OPERATION OF VEHICLE

MECHANIC'S SIGNATURE_____
DATE _____

The sleeper can be as big as 340 cubic feet of space (up to 8 feet high and 6 feet, 2 inches deep). The biggest sleepers have room for a bed, refrigerator, TV, VCR, microwave, laptop computer, storage space for clothes, sink, and toilet. Some of the biggest sleepers even have room for two bunk beds. Park at a truck stop or rest area to sleep.

TRUCK STOP

Take time out for breakfast at the truck stop. Truck stops are convenient places to shower and eat.

CB RADIO

Use the citizens band (CB) radio to talk to other truckers about traffic conditions and weather reports. The trucker's CB radio channel is #19. The emergency channel is #9.

On the road again...

Trucker Talk

anchor it: apply brakes for an emergency stop

barefoot: crossing a mountain pass without chains on the tires

hammer down: move fast, foot to the floor

roll and rest: when a long-haul driver drives and stops to sleep at regular intervals

gear bonger: trucker who grinds gears when shifting

chicken coop: weigh station

flip-flop: U-turn

monkey pickles: bananas (dark green when shipped)

backhaul: return load. After delivering a load of cargo, the trucker usually picks up another load that needs to be delivered somewhere close to headquarters.

motion lotion: diesel fuel, also called "go juice"

double nickel: 55 miles per hour

alligator: big hunk of rubber tread peeled off a truck tire, found on the side of the road

bark from the stacks: backfire from muffler

grunt for the grades: enough horsepower to get up steep hills with a heavy load

hundred-mile coffee: very strong coffee

bobtail: a tractor only, no trailer

covered wagon: trailer with sides and tarp

wiggle wagon: a tractor pulling double or triple trailers

skateboard: flatbed trailer

shiny hiney: trailer with stainless steel back door (Truckers don't drive close to these at night because headlights reflect back brightly.)

big rig: tractor-trailer

eighteen-wheeler: tractor-trailer with 18 wheels

four-wheeler: car

kiddie car: school bus

smoke him: pass another vehicle

bird dog: radar detector

coffin: sleeper compartment in the tractor

pigtail: light line used to transmit electrical power to trailer

break the unit: unhitch the tractor from the trailer

jump the pin: miss the kingpin when hitching tractor and trailer

10-4: "yes" or "OK" on the CB radio

10-20: trucker's location ("What's your 10-20?")

10-33: traffic due to accidents, natural disasters, and emergency vehicles such as ambulances and fire trucks

10-36: a call for the correct time ("What's the 10-36?")

ratchet jaw: trucker who talks too much on the CB

mud duck: very weak radio signal

brush your teeth and comb your hair: be on best driving behavior and within speed limit, because state trooper is approaching

bear: state trooper, also called "Smokey Bear"

bear bait: anyone driving over the speed limit

bear bite: a speeding ticket

feed the bears: pay a speeding ticket

bear den: state trooper station or headquarters

bear in the air: helicopter highway patrol, also called "spy in the sky"

bear in the bushes: state trooper hiding with a radar gun

front door: in front of the truck, as in "You've got a bear's den about two miles on your front door"

back door: behind the truck, as in "You've got a bear on your back door"